Talitha Koum!

"Little girl, I say to you, Arise!"

Reflections of a Girl Who Met Jesus

Cricket Aull, SFO

Talitha Koum
Author Cricket Aull, SFO
Copyright © 2009, Cricket Aull, SFO

Cover Image: Jeff West
Cover and book design: Mary Farag - Tau Publishing Design Department

Scripture quotations are from
THE REVISED STANDARD VERSION and the NEW AMERICAN BIBLE.

No part of this publication may be reproduced, stored in a retrieval system or transmitted in any form or by any means, electronic, mechanical, photocopying, recording, or otherwise, without written permission of the publisher.

For information regarding permission, write to:
Tau Publishing,
Attention: Permissions Dept.
1422 East Edgemont Avenue
Phoenix, AZ 85006

ISBN: 978-1-935257-49-3

First Edition, 2010
10 9 8 7 6 5 4 3 2 1

Published by Tau Publishing, Phoenix, AZ
For reorders and other inspirational materials visit our website.

Tau-publishing.com
Words and Works of Inspiration

Talitha Koum!

Arise and Pray 9

Arise in Peace 17

Arise in My Strength 23

Arise in Faith 31

Arise and Carry the Cross 37

Arise and Follow Me 45

Arise in Lowliness 53

Arise in Me 59

Arise and Serve 65

Arise in My Love 71

*S*cripture tells us that a twelve year old girl met Jesus under very unusual circumstances — He brought her back to life after she had died.

*B*ut we are not told any more about her. We don't know what this extraordinary experience meant to her, or how this shaped her life later on.

*T*ake a slow walk with her as she tells you about her encounter with the one who said to her,

"Arise."

"One of the synagogue officials, named Jairus, came forward. Seeing Jesus he fell at his feet and pleaded earnestly with him, saying, "My daughter is at the point of death. Please, come lay your hands on her that she may get well and live." He went off with him, and a large crowd followed him and pressed upon him... While he was still speaking, people from the synagogue official's house arrived and said, "Your daughter has died; why trouble the teacher any longer?" Disregarding the message that was reported, Jesus said to the synagogue official, "Do not be afraid; just have faith." He did not allow anyone to accompany him inside except Peter, James, and John, the brother of James. When they arrived at the house of the synagogue official, he caught sight of a commotion, people weeping and wailing loudly. So he went in and said to them, "Why this commotion and weeping? The child is not dead but asleep." And they ridiculed him. Then he put them all out. He took along the child's father and mother and those who were with him and entered the room where the child was. He took the child by the hand and said to her ...."[1]

Talitha Koum!

"*Talitha koum!*" I heard the words. But even more, I *felt* the words, as though they were summoning my whole being to come forth. I wonder now if this may be the summoning our souls experience when we are first called forth into life. Though this was a different matter for me. I was being called *again* to life, and the words I heard came upon me with such authority and such love, I immediately responded. I don't know if I could have done otherwise. There was something about these words and this voice that penetrated the deepest part of my being and I could not, nor did I wish to, deny its command. I arose.

The commotion around me was a blend of awe, delirium, amazed excitement … and … slight confusion on my part. My parents were hugging me and crying tears of joy. For myself, though, I was awestruck by the man in front of me. Kindness, wisdom, strength, peace, and understanding were in his eyes and in his voice, very much I would say, in his whole presence. I had never met anyone like him before.

That was the beginning of our bond, a deeply imbedded 'knowing' that I could talk with him about anything, the way a young girl would talk to her father, or a beloved uncle or elder brother whom she loved and trusted most in the world. "I am so blessed," I thought to myself, "that I have had this extraordinary encounter." It was clearly an encounter that I wanted never to end. Of course, many other people wanted an encounter with him as well, and he was seen almost always with a crowd of followers. So, for many days after this my heart was broken that I could not continue seeing him in the privacy of our home as it was on that first day he summoned me to arise.

Talitha Koum!

But I discovered over time that I *could*, in fact, continue this special bond of friendship. In my prayer time I would pour out my heart to God, and He would answer me, summoning me anew. An inner voice would come – not a voice I heard audibly – but I did, nonetheless, *hear* it. And it came from the same heart, the same gentleness, the same wisdom, compassion, peace, and love ... and with the same authority: *"Talitha koum"*- I would hear in the night – *"Little girl, I say to you, arise .... Arise now and pray!"*

Prayer, you see, keeps this friendship alive and present in my heart. Though many years have passed since I was a twelve year old girl, I still look forward to our times of quiet communion, when my heart and mind are directed to Him without distraction. He fills me anew with His presence then. He instructs me or He comforts me, or we simply sit in a silent expression of love. On some occasions He corrects me, but always with such loving compassion that the words are uplifting at the same time they admonish, and my heart is filled with a great desire to improve myself and grow in love. This, then, is a diary of our conversations together, in those quiet times of solitude and prayer.

Arise and Pray

Arise my daughter, arise now and pray.

Many mornings I have awakened to this familiar call upon my heart, and I arise from my bed at His bidding. At first, those were the only words I heard, but when He spoke, I could feel His sweet presence of love, and a profound peace would fill my room *and* my heart. I would pray, then, for the needs of people I knew or particular burdens I held inside, revealing only to Him my longings. He always understands such things!

I think it began in this way – His heart listening to everything that was in my heart. But at some point, I began to understand that if *I* listened to *Him*, even more was accomplished. Many of my burdens were lifted, or my prayers changed in focus. My thoughts and intentions were filled with new purpose. Prayer became a time of learning how to be still and open my heart to listen.

That is how I first began to hear His words to me.

Talitha Koum!

My daughter, I have much to say to you – if you would lay aside every distraction and every care. Your concerns cause a block in the flow of My blessings – not when you come to be alone with Me; you are learning to put all things aside then. But as you go through your day, as you meet with people and are confronted with responsibilities - even then, learn to turn all to Me with perfect peace that I am here to answer and provide for your needs. I am calling you to learn these things so you may walk in My presence daily – hourly – not just at these times of quiet prayer. Would you meet each person, each situation, each trial, each problem with expectant joy for the way I am guiding you? I promise to never leave you or forsake you – that means at each moment I am here. Turn everything into a prayer, with thanksgiving, for the resurrection power that has authority over your life. Trust and love – even when you don't understand. I am working all things together for your good. Live in this joyful revelation and others will see and want to know Me. This knowledge is held within My thoughts and words which you receive as the mind of Christ. Learn, my daughter, to walk in this - so you will see my resurrection graces follow everything you do.

I pray very much for God's guidance and grace, and for the docility my heart needs to enable Him to work. I pray because I am learning that faith in Him opens the way for greater things to happen. Was it not my own father's faith that spoke to Jesus saying, "Come lay your hands on her that she may get well and live"? I wonder how many opportunities we miss by not inviting the Lord to come and meet us in our need.

Arise and Pray

One morning, very early, I heard His calling to my heart, and I sensed that He wanted to instruct me. So I arose to wait upon Him and listen.

Bring to Me all that I bring to you in your day – each person, each situation, each question that arises, each course of action to take, each thought that comes, each desire of your heart, each moment, each breath.

"How can that be done?" I questioned. I wondered if I would get anything accomplished if I had to be so focused on every moment I was in. But He explained to me that He was speaking of a focus on *Himself*.

It is done deliberately at first, and then it comes very naturally, as your longing becomes more and more to be one with Me. Understand, though, that this longing is already inside of you, as it comes from My own longing, and I placed this within you as My gift of love when you were created. But now the remaining portion is for you to long for it yourself and cultivate it through prayer and seeking and the practice of emptying yourself of temporary and passing desires. Always seek out the eternal good that your present moment is already designed to bring. Seek Me and live. So few do this wholeheartedly, but for those who desire it, the way is opened.

Lord, if You show me how to pray and seek after You, I will try, but I need much more strength to live this call with my whole heart and attention. I do not know how to be emptied of myself so that I can live completely in You.

Know that I am leading you in this way. One day at a time – then one hour at a time – then one minute, and so on, until I have brought you to the present, moment-by-moment, of living in Me. Rejoice and be glad. I love you with an everlasting – always abiding – and ever-present love.

Talitha Koum!

I am beginning to learn, though very slowly, that each moment is a special and graced interaction with Him. This interaction is dear to the Lord, and I have the choice to use this grace and prayerful union, or ignore it. Prayer is a gift and a privilege we are given to stay near to Him.

> Lord, I give You the present moment and all moments of my life. I am so grateful to have Your love without fail, at all times. Your loving guidance and Your mercy fill me with all I need. Thank You for Your ever-present love.

I must explain, though, that one morning I heard His voice awaken me from a very deep slumber and I simply did not want to rise. I felt not only exhausted, but physically ill from my lack of sleep. In my heart, I so love those words when I hear them, *"My little one, arise. Arise now and pray."* But this time, I did not think I had the strength to get up. I was reminded then to focus on His words rather than my physical feelings. I managed to get out of bed and on my knees. He began:

The vessel I will use must be freed and emptied of self.

As He continued, I began to feel a little stronger.

Come to Me – all who thirst, all who are weary, all who mourn, all who suffer, all who are denied of love and peace, comfort and hope. Will you not come to Me and let Me give you rest? Why do you cling to things that cannot give you life – why not come to Me - Who is - all life? I will show you how: Believe in Me, that is how. Put faith in My presence, faith in My power, faith in My action of love. Your choices are faith-filled, or else they are self-filled. Which do you choose? If you would but realize the emptiness of self.

> Lord, I am trying to learn how to set myself aside, examine my actions, and choose that which will draw me nearest to You. Please help me to live immersed in Your love. Let me rely always on Your strength, Your wisdom, and Your holy guidance.

Prayer, as I said, is a gift and a privilege. Even when we might feel discouraged in our prayers, as I have felt myself many times, we should never forget that good will come from our efforts. These words of our heart and soul have a powerful effect when they are spoken with meaning and purpose and the purity of good desire. When we pray, our prayers not only reach out to God, they have a way into the hearts of people, a way we cannot reach with our outspoken words. I understood this to be so after a gathering of people in which I heard someone playing very beautiful music.

The people were gathered, but not for any music. They were arguing over a matter of little importance. It just happened that someone there began to play very sweetly upon a lute. The music was so soothing that one couldn't help but let it also sooth our souls as we listened. I noticed then, that even the people who were not, at first, wanting to hear music, were able to listen and be touched by it. For all who were present, the music worked its beautiful peace upon our hearts. Peace was received because peace was needed, and music provided the way. The same, I understand, is true of prayer. A person may not be expecting prayers or even wanting them, but when sincere and heartfelt prayers are said, the soul receives them, because they are needed. The healing, soothing, prayers are like beautiful music. And just like a calming melody, the words of petition and praise are 'heard' in an interior way. The very words we may not be able to 'speak' to another person, can be received through the pure intentions of our heartfelt prayers.

This is why we do not simply go through the motions of prayer or say the words without our heart and thought in it. We pray from our heart into God's heart, and those prayers do not return void.

Talitha Koum!

Today I was beseeching God and asking fervently for Him to make my heart, and the hearts of all people, to be more desiring of His will, and more desiring of His whole likeness to live within us. This seemed to be a great burden inside of me, and I prayed as if I needed to convince the Lord of this need. But He answered me with these words:

Am I not already desiring that Myself? Trust in what I am doing and in what I will do. Keep faith alive in your heart. Then, as you develop this truth in your mind, your heart, and your faith, you will see more and more how I am working to fulfill that good. Do not think you are without help or hope when I am so ready and desiring to provide all that is needed for your growth and well-being. It is not you who have chosen Me, but I who have chosen you, and created you for a holy purpose. Live in My kingdom and draw others to Me. My hope, My love, My peace reigns – come dwell in Me.

The Lord reminds me many times that He helps us, cares for us, and is already desiring to do the good that we need. I pray that my faith and love for Him increases so that I constantly allow Him to work unhindered in my life.

When I was a little girl I loved to hear my father tell me stories about our people and the mighty ways God intervened for their safety and need. Stories about Abraham and Isaac, and Moses, Elijah, and King David were fascinating to me and I wanted to hear them over and over. One of my favorites was the story of Joshua and the battle of Jericho. My father would relay the events to me in great detail and with lively actions. Of course, the best part was when the horn was blown and the people of Israel began to shout, and the walls of the city crumbled to the ground! Hearing my father tell these stories would replay in my mind many times over, and I think it instilled a great anticipation in my heart for what God would do for us. My father ended all of these stories reminding me how important it is to thank and praise God in all we need to accomplish. And so, from the time I was a little girl, I learned to sing my way through any chores I had. I sang the little psalm I was taught: *"I will bless the Lord at all times, His praise shall continually be in my mouth."*

Now I have learned that thanking God is still important in what we want to accomplish. It is a vital part of prayer, even before we see an answer to our prayers. I learned this as a child, and I still see that it is true.

"O magnify the Lord with me and let us exalt His name together." [2]

Prayer, I am learning, is more than the words we speak. Prayer occurs in all we do as we direct our actions and intentions to God throughout the day. He wants to be a part of everything we do. He is teaching me that our prayers to Him are very powerful. They are meant to affect every minute of our day. We are meant to make Him present to our needs and to the whole world, through our prayerful interaction with Him. Prayer is truly a precious gift and privilege we have been given.

One night especially, I remember feeling most discouraged over a need I had prayed for repeatedly. When I opened my heart to the Lord, He calmed me with these words:

My child, you have thought many times that your prayers have gone unanswered when you did not see the work that was being done through them. Learn to not look so much for the physical manifestations. It is in the spirit that the mightiest works are done. Though you do have needs to pray for in the physical realm, the deeper work, the eternal manifestations, are always in the spiritual; and though you cannot see it, you will one day realize how perfectly all your heartfelt prayers were answered.

Talitha Koum!

Thank you, Lord, for this profound gift of prayer. I hope to always pray with true faith and charity in my heart, and to one day see that I used this gift in a way that was pleasing to You and continually helpful to others.

A psalm of David's says,
"Let every one who is godly offer prayer to thee." [3]
I pray, Lord, that we would all offer prayers
of loving gratitude to You.
Help us to become godly and allow us
to honor You with lives that are
faithful to Your Word.

Arise in Peace

*Arise My daughter. Arise now in My peace.
I want to speak to you of My holy presence of peace,
so that you can share this peace with those who need it.*

I think I awoke all the more eagerly this morning, because I had fallen asleep with a joyful anticipation in my heart that the Lord might awaken me to pray. I look forward to the whispers of His voice upon my heart, and to those quiet times we spend alone in prayer. Perhaps, this time, I thought, He would speak to me about the longing in my heart to be one with Him at all times – even in my times of trial and conflict. He knew, of course, what was in my heart.

I am the place of peace you seek. Do not allow the troubles of the world to distract you from My presence, little one. The gift I give you in My holy presence cannot be taken away – but you can choose to step away from it. Bring into My presence all your cares and the cares of your loved ones. Bring to Me every weight that burdens you. Bring to

Me your daily duties, but do not leave My presence to worry over matters that only I can correct. Bring My dwelling – the kingdom of peace – with you to others, and help bring forth My peace by your attentiveness to Me. Speak of Me, and do not be afraid. I am here.

Lord, I want to live in the way You describe to me. I want to not be distracted by problems and conflicts. But at times, they weigh heavy on my heart and do not leave my mind. Please let me be filled with Your grace. Help me to trust that You are here with me in all circumstances.

As much as I am aware of the Lord's peace when I am in prayer, I still find that leaving this prayerful presence to handle other things causes me to lose the peace I had received. I question why I have to leave His presence at all. But I do not know how to maintain it.

Lord, it seems when I am most challenged, it is most difficult to remember the peace You have placed within my heart.

Align yourself to My Word and stay in My presence. Children of the Most High God – why do you leave Me in your thoughts to dwell upon things of the world, when those earthly things do not glorify Me and do not draw you to My side? Listen to My heart of love and good will. Dwell in My thoughts, as the whole heavenly host does, and be at peace, because I am peace and My way is peace. Learn to stay in My presence with your thoughts and your will. All will be well in the end. Use this time to learn and wait and pray. How much I love My children.

Arise in Peace

I am trying, Lord, to understand and carry out in my heart all that You explain to me. I am thankful You are so patient. I am learning that it is You I am supposed to keep in my thoughts. It is You I am supposed to keep in the forefront of my intentions and focus. If I concern myself with those things You are telling me, instead of the worldly way things appear, I believe I will discover Your presence in uninterrupted ways. I want to be pleasing to You and dwell in the peace Your holy presence offers us. Thank You for Your gift of peace.

I continue to puzzle over this journey of faith at times. I cannot seem to take the blessings I receive from the Lord in our time together and let that carry me through the trials that follow. In particular, I was questioning a recurring situation that always makes me fall back into doubt and anxious worry. I see the same fear that I had in the past, though I know I should have 'outgrown' that lack of confidence in the Lord by now. It seems I cannot simply forget and move on. I brought this to the Lord in prayer.

Child, bring your self more presently to Me. Moment by moment come to My heart of love and mercy, wisdom and guidance. I do not want you ill with worry or down trodden with dismay. I love My children and they never leave My heart. I do provide. This is a great journey for you – as it is for all who continue to follow My Word. Peace is yours, as I secured this for you on earth. What troubles your heart – leave to My care. What troubles your understanding – leave to My wisdom. Know that what is to come will usher in peace – so remain in peace. Bring others to finding their peace in Me.

My Lord, I thank You for Your peace, for being our peace, and for calling us to live in peace. Let me remember that peace is possible even throughout the struggles of our day.

Talitha Koum!

I know that I am learning from God's guidance in my life. I am thankful that He teaches me, and I am grateful for our times together when I can pour out my heart to Him for comfort. But sometimes I pray and there is only silence. Then I fall back into doubt and confusion. I make progress, only to find myself back where I was last month or last year.

> Lord, will I ever grow so close to You that I feel Your presence in my heart continually? Will I ever come close enough to hear Your voice always in my heart in place of these silent times?

Not immediately did the Lord answer me. I prayed and sought consolation many times in His presence. There must be a great purpose in His silence and in our waiting and seeking. Do we listen more attentively after waiting so long? Do our hearts make room for a deeper understanding after we have surrendered more completely to His mystery? How often I find myself refusing to wait or choosing not to surrender, as though dwelling on the problem is a better solution than waiting on the Lord. I prayed for guidance.

> Lord, help us find the way to You in all our needs.

Late that night, when I was awaked to pray, the Lord filled my heart with this 'answer' to my earlier thoughts of the day. He did not speak in words, as I sometimes hear, but in a comforting and clear 'knowledge' that I would describe in this way:

We should not be discouraged when silence seems to be the only answer to our prayers. Even in the silence, something is happening. Our heart is turned to Him – and His love, which is all good and generous to us, is not denying us what we need. It is sufficient, at those times, to simply be held in His love. Perhaps, after such a silence, we are even more aware, and appreciative, for the times He speaks more clearly. We can cherish those times, and be grateful for all the abundant ways He conveys His love to us.

Thank You, Lord, for the gift of love-filled silence. Your love is deeper than we can understand or imagine, so silence must sometimes be the only way You can breathe Your love into our hearts. I receive, Lord, and I thank You.

Sometimes peace comes to us not in the answer we wanted, but in a deeper purpose God intends for us to receive. An example of this was a time that I was very ill for many weeks, and though I prayed continuously for healing, it did not come. Finally, I did receive God's peace as my healing, for He explained to me:

What you are learning in the duration of this is far more important than the healing you await. Be patient, as time brings all these things to completion.

———

I did wait and I trusted, with the peace of God's holy purpose working as needed in my soul. May we all learn to be docile in His hands as He does what is best.

I see sometimes that I am not the only one who struggles to maintain a peace-filled heart. But recently I have wondered if we sometimes cling, in a way, to our sorrows or worry. I have caught myself talking repeatedly about my own problems. But I did not notice this tendency until I heard it coming from someone else. And in one incident, I sensed that the other person did not want to think very long of God or dwell on His goodness. I spoke of this in my prayers to the Lord.

Talitha Koum!

I realize my error, Lord, in focusing on my problems in place of You. I am learning to do better. But why, today, could I not encourage my friend to dwell on Your great goodness?

Some would rather cling to their own sorrows than be comforted by My peace. They ask for peace, but do not seek Me for it. They refuse My words and discard My instruction. All who know Me must be a great witness, a true and steady light in the darkness of the world. I will never leave you or forsake you. I do not forsake any who come to Me truly in their heart. It is My heart that saves. Give up your heart – your self-centered longings. All life is in Me. All peace and all compassion are present in My heart of love. How much I love My people. Do not waver from showing them the truth of My peace and My presence.

I have come to understand now, through His words of peace, that I must recognize at the very start, when the peace He gives me begins to leave my heart. At the first sign of anxious worry, when I am confronted by something that causes fear or doubt, it is then that I can – and consciously should – bring myself back to the remembrance of His holy and peaceful presence. When I do so, His words of peace fill me again. In this way, I need to constantly 'guard' the place of peace He gives me, and bring myself back to it when that sacred place has been threatened.

Lord, when there is heaviness on my heart and mind, I will recall Your peace and bring myself back to this dwelling place of Your presence. Thank You for the grace that enables me to do so.

I offer to the Lord, then, all areas of my life that are in need of His peace. I offer these needs with faith in His love and with repeated meditations on His peace-filled presence. Thank You, Lord, for providing the peace my life needs now and in time to come.
Thank you for the calm of Your presence.

Arise in My Strength

Arise, My daughter. Arise in My strength and be encouraged. You are much closer to Me when you deny your self-focus than you realize.

He was speaking to me about the struggle I was having as I tried to fast. I felt like I was failing because it was so hard. Then He repeated to me from the prophet Zechariah: "Neither by force nor by strength, but by my spirit! says the Lord of Hosts." He let me ponder these words for awhile, then He continued:

Learn in every circumstance how to go deeper into My presence. Can you not see, after all this time, that there is more?

Bring to Me everything – everything – everything. That is the way to transformation. Recognize what is of self, and give it to Me. It may seem the smallest, most insignificant matter, but you do not recognize its weight in the spiritual realm. Give it to Me.

Talitha Koum!

Just as you have learned to give your lack of peace to Me at the first sign of its leaving, so now, give all to Me that is not of Me at the first recognizable sign. I will help you with every trial.

> Lord, some of my trials are so difficult. They are greater than I can handle. I try to overcome my self-focused weakness, but it seems I always fall again.

Your difficulty to deny yourself comes from relying on your own strength. My strength is your only strength. My moment of grace is all you need.

You try, instead, to find strength against the entire temptation. If you would simply see the trial in the small step-by-step process before you. You have My grace in the very measure you need. See Me with you in everything. That is how to enter My peace. That is the way to receive my strength. That is how you will know that I am with you, never forsaking your need of Me. Live in My kingdom step by step and moment by moment. I make all things new in this way.

> Lord, I ponder Your strength. I ponder Your glory and Your goodness. Let me ponder You in place of my problems, and praise You in place of my repeated focus on fears and doubt. I want to trust in You at all times, Lord. Help me in my times of failure to return to You and try again with greater faith and determination. Thank You for Your strength that never fails us.

> Some people, Lord, seem to follow You so easily. They seem to trust without question and continue on the path of faith without wavering. Lord, I want that same depth of faith. I want to be completely surrendered to Your will and Your leading. Teach me how to live without resistance to You.

Arise in My Strength

How sweet were His words to me then, explaining how to live as one with Him:

You will have no resistance when you realize that you have no life apart from Me. You are moved by desires, child. Desires that you have placed in your heart from past pleasures or future longings. When your whole heart and all your thoughts are filled with longing for Me and My desires, you will be moved by love – perfect love coming from the Father – through Me – and empowered by My Holy Spirit. Apart from Me you can do nothing. See how you, of yourself, are in total need, but see, even more, how you are loved beyond measure and held in My hands. I am ready to lead you into all life. Live in union with Me.

   Please explain to me, Lord, how to live in union with You.

Learn to see Me always with you, as the One who adds life and dimension to all you do. Without Me nothing has life. You must learn to remain small and creatable in My hands. It is not you, but I, who give life. Apart from Me you can do nothing.

   Then how, Lord, shall I see myself as small and creatable?

By faith – by desire – and then by choice, which is your free will to be in My care. Do you see the pattern here? Your faith has to lead from the longing in your heart, then your free will chooses to step in that direction. If your faith is not in Me, you will trust in your own poorly lit judgment. If your heart and soul do not long for My will, you will be distracted and misguided. But your will – will be determined by what your faith is able to trust in and your heart is longing to do. Apart from Me you can do nothing. How much I have in My hands for you to do, how much in My will. Let My love carry you.

   Lord, let me learn what it is to be willing to follow You. When I try to do this, I seem to have so little strength.

Let Me be your strength, child.

Talitha Koum!

How am I to understand what this means, Lord? I respond with the strength I have inside, how do I let You be that strength?

Child, you must live immersed in Me. Let the part of you that is deeply connected to Me, that which is spirit-given-life, by My Spirit – let that come forth to live. Rely on Me, not on your strength, not your own perception. Take My life – My perception – My strength. Learn at each moment what it is to set yourself aside and allow Me to live in you. There is no strength apart from Me – no life apart from Me.

Lord, thank You for faith that allows me to trust in Your love. I give You my heartfelt longings and ask You to inspire me with greater love to live according to Your will. Even in difficult situations, Lord, make it my desire to be one with You.

I need, so much, Your forgiveness, Lord. Please revisit me with Your grace. Help me to make better choices when trying situations come.

I was struggling with an old, revisited area of self-pride. I can often tell in the middle of my choices that I am going in a less desirable direction than I should. But on this occasion I ignored the promptings of heavenly help and let my worldly impulses dictate my actions. That evening, I deeply regretted it and I stayed in prayer awhile longer, asking for forgiveness.

I prayed and worried over my poor choices of that day, until it became clear to me that I needed to stop dwelling on my mistakes and enter the help of His presence. There He spoke to my heart:

Arise in My Strength

I give you every opportunity to turn away from sin and overcome it. If your heart finds delight in the temptation that is before you, learn to turn your gaze to Me immediately – call on the Holy Spirit and walk ever so close to Me like a child that is in the dark. Soon, after a carefully guided calculation-of-steps, I will lead you back into the light and you will be stronger for having made the journey.

Temptations are allowed for your soul to grow in purity, after having the impurities, however small, brought to the surface and exposed to the light. Then you are able to work with grace to make the victory your own. In this way, you are 'owning' the victory I have made possible for your soul to attain. Use every opportunity I am supplying for your growth in Eternal Love.

My Lord, how faithful You are! I want to always remember that You are near to me and realize the help You are providing. Help me, please, to recognize the good You are doing in my heart as I go through trials and learn to overcome them with Your grace. Will I ever learn these things? I want to live in You and follow the promptings You place in my heart to help me make worthy choices.

Days later, He continued to speak to me about the importance of seeing myself as a child:

A little child has free will, but is powerless to carry it out when the choice is something that requires greater strength and knowledge than the child can possess.

Yes, I thought – a child can only do so much on its own. If this small one chooses to do something wrong – those who are bigger and stronger can easily intervene. And if the child chooses to do something very good, the assistance of someone older is still often needed.

Talitha Koum!

Can you not see yourself as a child in this way? You are powerless to carry out your desire to do what is good. But at each step of the journey you can come to Me for strength, and at each step I will be faithful to provide what you need. You must take the smallest step before you – the one step you can do. I will make you capable of each new step as it comes. Be patient with yourself and with others. I am working these things together for your good.

>Thank you, Lord. I will take the small step I am capable of making, and then ask – and trust – in Your strength to go further. Thank You for providing, and for sustaining me, in all my needs. I am Your child. I trust in You.

I must describe another time I was deepened in my understanding of the Lord's strength. I was awakened early from a very deep sleep and I felt extremely tired – too tired to get up for prayer, but I sensed I was not supposed to stay in bed. I struggled for awhile with this recurring thought that I was being asked to get up to pray. I wanted only to sleep. And then I heard Him say:

The best time to conquer the flesh is right at the beginning of resistance. Don't wait for a better time to try to defeat the temptation that is before you.

I got out of bed, ignoring my body's want for sleep, and began to pray. I do not know how long I prayed, though it did not seem long before I was able – by His grace – to embrace the Lord's presence completely. And just as I reached that interior place of devotion, love, and abandonment, I suddenly felt a complete peace overcome me entirely, so that even my physical body was no longer tired and sick, but alert, and completely united to the Lord's request of me. And just as this happened, I heard the words:

Arise in My Strength

People are often defeated in their spiritual battles because they do not let Me lead them, but they desire to follow instead, the ways of their flesh and self-attention. Remember this - all is provided for you to advance in spiritual perfection.

I saw, then, what looked like two battlefields, though I knew them to be of a spiritual sense. The first, and smaller, was each individual's own battlefield and regarded the discipline of conquering the self. The second battlefield was the Lord's, and signified His complete victory over sin and death. I saw how very interconnected these two battlefields were.

But I also saw a serious misunderstanding: We too often try to enter the second battlefield without facing our 'self' on the first one. We want what the Lord has attained for us, without denying our own will in order to receive it. A free gift has been given us by the Lord, but to partake in the richness of its blessings, we need to give up our will for His which is divine.

"The Lord is my strength and my shield." [4]
The psalms often speak to us about the Lord's strength.
I will think upon this today, and recount
'the wonderful deeds the Lord has done' in my life.
How often, Lord, You have been my strength,
my shield, and my saving help,
without my awareness or gratitude.
Thank You, O my God!

Arise in Faith

*Arise now in faith. I am calling you to deeper faith -
and greater surrender.*

What an exercise this journey of faith is! I seek the Lord, I learn from His words, and yet, I still struggle to put them all into practice. Just as I seem to be making progress, I realize how far I must be from truly loving and giving myself - and my will - to God.

How, Lord, am I to view this current situation? So many pressures make it hard to keep my focus on You. I feel myself wavering and ready to fall. Will You be my stronghold in this time of trouble?

Child, I am calling you to great trust. Faith in Me — abandonment to My will — will sustain you. My loved ones would be so safe, if they were able to trust. I offer all that is pure and holy and humble as your place of refuge. Do not be distracted from the holy dwelling place of My presence. Learn to stay close to Me. Learn to walk and talk

and breathe My presence. People will choose My love or worldly ambitions. Do not be distracted with worldly allurements. I am here with you — how vital to begin seeing that now, before the trials of life add greater difficulty to the choices you must make.

Lord, I am grateful for Your patience and Your guidance on my behalf. I want to see You and serve You without distraction. I am beginning to think, though, that You do not want to simply remove these worldly distractions from me. Are You, instead, wanting me to learn how to outgrow and overcome them? I need all Your help to do this, as You know. I trust in You to lead me.

There has been a great burden carried in my heart these days. Like David's psalm, I ask, "How long, O Lord, wilt thou look on?" God's help is hard to see right now; but His help is my only hope. I do not know how to get through this otherwise. The Lord comforted me with these words:

I am going to move on your behalf. Trust Me little one. Do not be anxious over your lack of control in this situation, for I am in control, not you. I am watching and waiting for the perfect timing of all things considered. It is not a time for you to feel in despair. Place your hope and trust in Me alone. Focus on the love I have shown you — already present around you in many ways. I love you My daughter, My precious one. Believe — trust and believe. I am only asking that which will bless you. Leave all to Me. I am going to move on your behalf.

I believe, Lord. But forgive me for my recurring fears and anxiety. This is a greater trial than I have ever carried. With Your help, I place myself into Your hands. I will await Your saving help and trust in You.

When the Lord calls us into greater trust of Him, I suppose it should not surprise us that the journey requires more faith or more determination than we previously had. His faithfulness to us does not change, I am sure of that. But our trust in His faithfulness must deepen and become even more confident.

Child, be with Me in all your moments of sorrow, anger, and frustration. If you will give Me full authority at those troubling times, it will allow the good - that was always planned - to come forth and bless. Be at peace, My little one. I am leading and working your trials for good. Faith is yours – use it to stay near and be untroubled. I calmed the sea when the storm arose and threatened the apostles. Know that I can calm every storm within yourself. I came that you might have life and have it abundantly. Receive My life. Be at peace, and know that I am God. All is well. I repeat – all is well.

———

Be with me, Lord. Let me grow ever more confident in Your love for me, and in Your constant, careful, watch over my needs. I ask You to calm the storms of my mind and heart right now. Thank You for Your love and Your peaceful presence. I know it will be sufficient to sustain me.

Talitha Koum!

The Lord gave me a beautiful teaching in my heart while I was with a friend. I was trying to encourage her to trust in God over a particular situation that was very distressing. As I was talking with her, I suddenly saw the Lord standing by her side, knowing the whole circumstance, just as she herself had experienced it. But there was a very big difference between His view and the way she perceived the matter. She saw the situation with much fear and only anticipated everything going from bad to worse. I saw that the Lord was seeing exactly the same situation, but with the assurance that everything would go from what it was now to something better. In His view there was nothing to fear. He was not worried because He saw the very answer to her needs. He knew how to work the entire circumstance around for a good purpose, and He was already setting particular people and situations in place to help her. Being God, He knew what was needed and was sending the proper provision.

I understood then, that this gift of faith we are given, gives us the ability to 'see' things with His perspective of hope. Even if we cannot see the events He is fore-planning, we can trust that He sees, and is providing, the most suitable solution. His *faithfulness* is what we can always 'see' with the eyes of faith. In this way we take on the same mind, or perspective, as Christ. We ask for His help to intervene and we work with the grace He provides. How much peace this gave, and continues to give, me.

There was another time the Lord confirmed this word to me of deepening my faith and seeing things with the hope He has provided. What hinders this, He explained to me, is human attachment. How important it is to be more attached to God and rise above attachments to the world. He explained it to me in this way:

You will know earthly attachments by the clinging they have to your desires, your thoughts, or your will. Recognize what power they wield on your poor soul that was created to cling to its Creator, though you, with fleshly desires, may prefer to cling to the world. Learn to recognize through stillness and prayerful attention, those indications that something other than your Lord is drawing you. You have, in the power of your will, only to make the choice – and I will be there with full and sufficient grace to aid you in your clinging to Me. But choosing the world allows the world to dictate your attachments.

As I have spoken to you before, your choices are faith-filled or else they are self-filled. Which do you choose?

Lord, I desire to choose You and Your ways in all of my life. Thank You for giving us truth and light for our journey of faith. Thank You for the example of others who have walked this way before us and show us how to cling to You and not to the world.

I have been examining in myself those times that I have a wrong focus, or wrong attachments. It seems they are often the same times that I have the most trouble denying my self-will in order to serve God's will. I see too often that I am more caught up in what I am doing than in my faith and love for Him. It is our love for the Lord, and His love for us, that should lead us in the direction of His grace. I am learning to focus on this.

I will show you what the appearance of holiness is like in the soul – it consists in nothing less than being wholly united to Me. Be one with Me in everything – and in your earthly attachments, let your soul only see them as impediments to your true calling – eternal life with Love. Let nothing separate you, even for a moment, from your true and holy joy which is union with Me.

Talitha Koum!

I stayed up late into the night after everyone else, it seemed, had gone to sleep. I had much to pray for, and many people on my heart to lift up to the Lord. Sometimes I feel that my own faith is kneeling before the Lord on behalf of others, for those who do not pray or do not know His great goodness for which they could pray. I began with wanting to carry these burdens to the Lord for those in need. But I became, instead, very heavy myself with all their troubles and I left my time of prayer feeling very discouraged. He said:

Listen, My child, wait and be still. Already the cares of the world are becoming too great a burden for many. If faith is not strong, if the house has not been established on a firm foundation, the weight of care and confusion will bring it down. Now, more than ever, let faith be strong and unshakable. Those who know Me will have to raise Me up for others to see and believe. Do not be distracted. I am your God; be careful not to replace My sacred place with something worldly. Keep Me in the center of your heart – your mind – and your will. Lead others in this way, and pray for hearts to receive. I say to you, do not let your heart be troubled, neither be dismayed. Believe in Me.

Lord, I do believe, and I am trying to believe even in times of care and confusion. You are the hope we believe in, the faithful One we trust, and the new life we need in our hearts. Teach us how to keep You at the center of our lives.

As I mediate on the innumerable ways God has
shown His faithfulness to me,
I become even more aware of His love and constant care
in my life. His faithfulness to me never ends.
So I thank You again, Lord,
and gratefully renew my faithfulness to serving You.

Arise and Carry the Cross

*Arise, My precious one,
and carry the cross of My love.*

I have heard, since I was a small child, that following the way of our Lord is not easy. I used to think that people who spoke this did not know the Lord as I did. He comes to me with such gentleness and love. But I have learned that it <u>is</u> *not easy*. When I was a child I did not know that following Him meant following His example – in all circumstances. How many times and circumstances require us to carry, for love of Him, a cross like His own.

Lord, I am so weary of this present suffering. Why are some people so cruel? Why do they not consider that their view of the situation may be very limited, even incorrect? When I try to help others it ends up hurting me. Why is it so difficult to follow this good path of love and faith?

Talitha Koum!

Look to Me when you suffer a trial, My child. Use this time to draw nearer and nearer to My heart and the image of My love. You become distracted by the circumstances, instead of letting the circumstances bring you to Me. It is here, at the cross, you will be fashioned into the image of love. Always let your heart be set on coming into My presence, closer and closer to Me at every moment. The sacrificial heart is precious to Me – it is opened to My holy will and led, assuredly, by the guidance and unity of Your God who is love.

Make us stronger, Lord, in following Your will. Help us to unite our trials to the cross and grow closer to Your likeness as we encounter difficulties. You were obedient in all things to Your Father. Help me to be obedient, as well, and to consider the holy call Your grace allows us to embrace.

More and more I find that people are going through difficult times. I hear about unexpected tragedies, health problems, fears for our safety. The trials of life seem greater and more fearful with each day. But the Lord instills upon my heart to not fear, to be at peace, and to trust in His Lordship over my life. He uses all things for a good purpose, I was told. I prayed for understanding to carry these burdens. He answered my questions with such wisdom, I was able to see His love in new ways – ways that turned my mind toward hope and confident faith. He tells us to trust. He is *not the cause* of our trials and suffering, but He is the one who *sustains us* through them and *uses all* for good. In faith we can believe that He is holding us, and doing something greater. With the gentleness of His heart, and words that allowed me to see more deeply, He said:

In the beginning, trials and sufferings will seem harsh and without meaning to the senses. But later, through prayer and yielding of yourself to My love, they draw you to My side in ways unseen to your eyes. Only your interior heart can lead as the 'self' learns to follow this perfect path of My holy bidding. You seem to be in the dark – but I am surely leading. Trusting surrender – as you have been told before – is your part. Do not be afraid along this path which is brightly lit from one side, though your side seems dim and barely lit to understanding. No matter – the course is assured. I will lead. The innermost place of your heart will follow. Pray and be at peace. The faculties you are so used to using do not comprehend this journey. The 'self' has to yield here, to the place of your soul's connection to God. Love knows the way. Faith knows to follow. Hope knows to persevere. The destination is secure. Happy are those who yield to this leading.

Lord, I am trying to understand, trying to grow in my trust of Your love and sovereignty. Only You can see the whole picture, and in Your holy and loving care, You intend that our trials be used to our benefit. When life gets very difficult, It is difficult to believe You are in authority. But I believe You know what is happening, I believe You can do all things, and I believe You love and care for us beyond our understanding. You walk at all times with us to help us. Please help me, especially at those times that I struggle to believe completely.

I have noticed a deepened sensitivity growing inside of me. It is like the deeply sensitive awareness I am learning to have for the Lord's presence, but this sensitivity seems to be for other people. Days ago, I was visiting a close friend at her home. I knew that she had experienced great difficulty in certain close relationships of her life. She had shared that with me on previous occasions. But on this day while at her home, at a moment that I was being still and prayerful, I was suddenly overcome with such sorrow, as though all of *her* sorrow was inside my own heart.

Talitha Koum!

I would have thought, by the presence of this sudden anguish, that *I* was going through something deeply painful, only I had no reason in my life to feel such pain. I wondered then, if I was being allowed to know *her* inner heart – the years of pain she had carried inside. My thoughts, then, went to Lord, who intimately shares in all of our sorrows. He does this so compassionately with each of us. We have the comfort of knowing that He has borne all our sufferings, and in such a way as to make those sufferings an instrument of holiness for us. His sharing in our lives is a tremendous gift.

Later that evening, the Lord gave me this explanation for His presence of love. As we draw closer to Him, we, too, are asked to share in His compassion for others, even His compassion that bears pain.

Are you willing to let Me take you more deeply into the suffering of My Sacred Heart – My heart which bears the pain of all who are in need – and for all who suffer? Are you willing to enter My own sorrow for those who do not know Me, or the plans I have for their lives, plans that are for good and not evil? I am sorrowful for those who do not know I have the answer for their needs. I have sorrow for those who reject the perfect will I have created them to fulfill. Be near to Me, daughter. Bear with Me these sorrows; and each time I let you near enough to feel them yourself, bear them with Me and comfort Me, for even yet, these souls can be turned to Me through prayer and sacrifice.

Lord, You are compassion and love. You are the kindness, the gentleness, and the faithfulness that longs to live in our hearts. Help me to come into Your heart of love, and to bear with You the love You have for others.

Soon after, He spoke to me again about bearing the sorrow that He holds in His heart for each person. He understands each heart and knows the struggles, the fears, the disappointments and the discouragement. He shares somehow that pain with us, and then invites *us* to *be like Him* in this miraculous *way of love*. I am beginning to understand my part as a participation *with Him*, as a way of uniting myself with His self-sacrificing love. United to Him in this way, He brings forth a transformation in the heart. But not only my own heart – in the heart of someone else as well, someone who's pain He has lovingly invited me to share. This, I think, is the truest example of love – it bears the pain of others for love of them. What a great gift this is! Though without this love that comes from Him, it is indeed a stumbling block to our understanding.

My child, I am calling many to bear My wounds at this time. Many will enter the sorrow of My Sacred Heart. Many will hear, as I hear, the cries of My needy ones. Tell them to bear with Me all that they suffer. Tell them to endure for love of Me what is troubling and painful. Tell them it is My cross they bear and My sorrowful pain they have come to know. But tell them, as well, that I love enough to bear all these wounds and, in love, bring forth healing, hope, and restoration for the world.

Tell them to endure for love of Me. I will transform the hardened hearts, the needy hearts, and the suffering hearts. I will work in ways that will amaze all who are watching, waiting, and praying – believing, even when the sorrow they have entered appears greater than the hope they have held on to. Do not allow your hearts to be downcast, but pray and persevere even more in your trials. Mercy is great at this time. Be instruments of My mercy and peace and loving patience. The world is being transformed through love – the love you have found in the cross. Let all who love enter into the life that will bear this cross with love and steadfast faith. Enter with Me. Believe and wait and pray, steadfast in your love.

Do not doubt that I have called you. And do not doubt that I am using all your trials for good. Love heals. Love transforms. Love endures and perseveres. Live in My love, knowing this will triumph in the end. Encourage one another.

Talitha Koum!

Lord, Your love is pure and perfect. Your love is beyond my understanding. But I know that Your love is true and faithful, so I give to You all of myself. Take possession of me with Your love, especially, Lord, at those times when the weariness of life and the trials of fear and suffering seem greatest.

How quickly I can fall after I had thought I turned to God and had given Him my life. I was so hurt yesterday by the words and actions of someone I thought to be a close friend. I had decided to shut myself off from any further contact. "I can do without people such as that in my life," I said to myself. And I was quite content to let very ill feelings begin to dwell in my heart. But the Lord came to me with these words:

Are you not willing to endure for love of Me these small wounds? I tell you, many people do not want the piercings of the heart that make their heart like Mine, or the piercing of their hands for doing My work, or the piercing of their feet that comes from walking the extra steps to show My love to others. Do not be afraid to receive into your heart My healing love from the cross – for love is needed to heal you and My whole Body.

Keep your eyes on Me, my child. And do not let current problems lead you out of My presence. See yourself with Me at, and in, all times. We walk through your life as one, with Me bearing the greater burden. People will use their trials and suffering to become more self-centered or more Christ-centered. Let them offer these trials for those who are without faith, and let them be joined to the work of redemption and transformation I bring to the world.

Lord, I place my hope and trust in You. Always You are there to guide me - a very present help in trouble. Forgive me for turning a hardened heart toward others. May I live this path of love You have shown me in a way that is pleasing to Your will.

Arise and Carry the Cross

The Lord gives me much to think about. When faced with so many trials of life, I want to remember that there is a true and holy way that is set before me, and it is contrary, in many respects, to our natural, worldly tendencies. A struggle with our flesh seems to be necessary to acquire a holier spirit. The Lord's cross becomes our own, and provides the way.

Should it surprise you, My daughter, that the closer you come to Me, the more you may come close to enduring a trial? And should it surprise you that the closer you come to enduring a trial, the more you will come close to Me? Let your heart, at all times, be open to the love that transforms; and by reason of needing transformation, may endure a trial, at times, to get there. Hope in My word of love. All will be offered the gift of transforming love. Embrace My love and pray for those who have yet to understand the gift being offered them. You still have need to be emptied, child, but continue on the path I bring before you each day. My grace is sufficient, My will provides.

> My Lord, I remember the words that Your prophet, Isaiah, spoke, that Your ways are not our ways. I pray that I can always be faithful to You, even when Your way is one my flesh needs but does not want to follow.

Shortly after this, I was feeling very burdened by constant struggles in my life. My problems, and those of many people I knew, seemed overwhelming. "Why so much hardship in everyone's life?" I questioned. The Lord then placed another word upon my heart for my encouragement:

Talitha Koum!

My wearied one, do not be surprised over the trials that are unfolding around you. Remember that in My plan, I use them all to give strength for the interior journey needed in one's soul. This is a time of peace, though it comes through turmoil, a time of hope, though it comes through hopeless-like situations. Do not lose faith. I am here to provide. I see all that is coming and I provide the means of life. Encourage others with your faith. Let them see your unfailing love for one another. Settle in your heart My perfect love and My sovereignty. I will never leave you or forsake you. Trust and believe. I will lead. Find great comfort in this promise – I will lead you.

I renew myself to You, Lord. I get discouraged by my many failures to carry Your holy cross with You. But You continually show me Your love and assist me again with Your strength. I trust in Your leading and I humbly follow.

Today I will reflect on the times that my own life
has been a participation with Christ
in His sorrow and compassion for others.
I want to grow more in the image and likeness
of Christ through these personal 'crosses' of my life.
Lord, I choose to unite my life to Yours
with more love and faithfulness.

Arise and Follow Me

Arise, My child. Arise and follow Me with a heart of faith, hope, and love.

What blessed things I have been shown. The Lord called to me, asking me to follow Him. But so gentle is His leading! I was first shown such profound thoughts of love, that following Him would be void of fear. I am learning to live without fear and walk in His love. These were His words of encouragement to me:

How much I love My people! See how I come to deliver you. I come to deliver from death, from sin, from evil, from self, from all that stands in the way of abundant life. Let Me reveal to you the wonders of living in My Spirit – the joy of walking in My will. Let Me give you a vision of abundant life: It is walking closely, so closely to My side, that we can talk freely. I whisper to your heart, and your heart, being eager to hear from Me, is ready to answer, "Yes, Lord" just as I always said "Yes" to My Father as He whispered to Me on the earth. Walk closely, find joy in the thought that I am leading you. Turn every thought, every longing, every anxious moment to My perfect care. Why do you hesitate

Talitha Koum!

to give Me all of your life? I love you and I want to care for you in the most perfect way. I will show you as we walk together – a joy here – a revelation there – a trial sometimes, but always a victory in the end. My love is perfect. Give all you have to Me. No greater love has anyone than the love the Father has for you through Me. Live every moment with that in mind.

What is this - that the Lord should love us so much that He walks with us and chooses to be a part of our lives so intimately? He desires to give us such favors from His heart and to bless us so richly with loving wisdom and care! How can we understand such goodness?

>   Help me, O Lord, to receive and be transformed by all Your gracious gifts, given out of such love!

For many days He spoke to me of following Him:

My child, why do you hesitate in coming to be with Me? I know your heart, I know all that is within your thoughts. You try to seek Me first, but you allow distractions and doubt to dissuade your path to Me. Be diligent for Me and for My Word. You have only begun to understand, and you hardly have touched the depth of My Words. Child, the time has come to be ready at every whisper I give to you, to act trustingly and obediently. Don't wait for someone else to do it – I have a task for you. In My divine plan, I have ordained events that begin with the smallest of seeds, a word, even a gesture, can lead to a life changing occurrence. But I need obedient and willing workers to carry out the work of My kingdom. This comes from hearts who have been prepared and purified and empowered to carry out My will. Make yourself ready.

Lord, You know my thoughts and all my ways. Nothing is hidden from You. I come before You again, asking for Your help to be faithful. Create in my heart a greater desire for this, Lord. I want to follow You at all times, but I need Your help even to do so.

I see so many needs in people's lives. It seems sometimes that I have little to offer them, but still, God is faithful to take my small offering and do much more with it. I often hold people in prayer when there is nothing more I can provide, and the Lord takes their hearts into His hands and blesses them far beyond my simple requests. It always amazes me to see how the Lord works, and how He uses my participation to fulfill His will.

You are truly reaching people you do not know and touching lives you have not yet seen. The work in My kingdom is hidden to this world, but will one day be revealed. Walk through this day with Me – we are making preparations for the kingdom. Let that be in your thoughts as you go through the hours of this day. Be attentive to My whisper – to My leading – as we make preparations for My kingdom.

———

I come, Lord. I come to listen and to follow. I come to be made ready by Your holy leading. I give You my hesitations and inhibitions as much as I am able to give them. You must lead and inspire me all along the way. Thank you for Your holy and perfect way, and for the gift of faith that allows us to trust in You, in place of our own understanding.

Talitha Koum!

Lord, I don't seem to know how to stay close to You, how to keep myself in the awareness of Your presence. I find myself going about many things throughout the day without even a thought of You. I want to know how to find You, and be a part of You, in all I am doing. Please help me. How can I be sure You are with me, when I do not feel I am with You as I should be?

Don't worry, My child. Truth is here and leads you. There is much to say – much to express in truth and heart, much that goes beyond words. Open your heart and sit with Me. Seek Me with all desire. Be still and wait, letting your desire reach deeper levels of longing and readiness. Listen with ears so attentive to My voice that distractions of the world have no weight and cannot interfere with the longing I have put into your heart to be one with Me. That is the posture, the attentiveness, the longing, that allows you to find Me.

After a long and prayerful silence, He continued:

My people hunger for Me, but many still allow the world to fill their appetites. Seek Me and you will find a treasure rich beyond the world's offerings. Today, learn to walk with listening ears, seeking heart, and longing will for Me; then you will find Me in your presence. Do not be discouraged when you think you have only 'unfeeling senses' or 'unhearing ears.' I led My people into the desert to find Me. Solitude, which few make time for, opens your senses to receive from My heart. My heart is full, so yours must be emptied to receive. My way is light, so your way must be seen as dark and lightless sometimes. I heal the sick. I bring light into darkness. I fill what is empty. That is how you can receive My presence. Be at peace that I am leading. I know the way. I am the way.

I think many times I fail miserably at following the Lord. In the psalms, King David wrote "I delight to do thy will, O my God." I need so much help from God to do the same.

Why is this so hard for me? I should want to be faithful to You, more than the enjoyment I get doing things as I choose. How can I grow in my desire to be obedient? I truly want to do better.

He spoke into my heart:
Find your joy in being obedient.

I have thought and prayed so often about my need in this; how do I find joy in obedience? I think obedience must be our way to joy because it allows our soul to grow closer to God. That should be our greatest joy. But I am still finding it hard in many ways, even if I know it is done for love of Him. My 'joy' does not simply come because I have chosen to do what I should.

He added this perspective then:

True joy is not self-centered, just as peace is not self-centered, but Christ-centered. Your peace, your joy, your life - is centered in Me. Do not grow weary in well-doing.

It seemed that all through the day, the Lord was giving me something more to think about in answer to my question.

Your key to the first step of obedience is this: keep your focus upon God and not yourself.

And when you have a choice between two things, choose the more humble.

He gave me time to wait and ponder more thoroughly each new thought and how it related to my understanding of obedience. Then He would continue.

Do not seek to dwell in the future as much as you seek being with Me in the present. Learn to find Me in the present moment; that is how you will learn obedience.

Talitha Koum!

This is very true, I am learning. More and more I realize the value, the grace, and the fruitful results we gain from living just in the moment we have with Him.

I confess, though, that in the present moment I notice that I am least humble, because that is when I most often choose to ignore the Lord's promptings and satisfy myself instead.

That evening in my prayer time, He added these words:

My love, My hope, and My peace will be found in the present moment. Learn to live with Me in each moment that is before you. In each moment is My holy presence, and therefore, each moment with Me is equipped with grace that is sufficient. Stay near to Me, even when you do not feel My presence with you. I am with you in greater ways than you can understand, more completely than you realize. Stay near to Me and receive all you need.

> Lord, I am grateful for Your presence of love and the promise of all I need. I will stay very near to You, but I know that I even need Your grace to do that. You are faithful to provide, what do I need to fear? I trust in You.

When the Lord calls us to follow Him, He means this to be a constant following – not only to go where He would go, but to also do as He would do and to become as He already is.

> Lord, I do not see how my small life could be the instrument of Your wonderful presence to those around me. But I pray that I could follow Your will and help those who need to find their way to You.

Arise and Follow Me

My faithful one, be the light that shows the way for the many who are in darkness now. Do not waver and do not hold back. I make the way in the wilderness, and for many, a wilderness is all they will see until their hearts are truly one with Mine. Show them My light of love and pray for them to receive it. How I love – how I love – how much I love My people. Do not waver from showing them the truth. I am with you always.

With Your grace, Lord, I will do this. I will make myself more present to You and to those You put into my life. Help me, please, to be for others the light of love You so graciously pour forth upon me.

And so I ask the Lord,
"How would you have me follow You?"
I offer to You, again, my humble life and I wait
upon You, Lord, for strength and guidance.
I thank You for being faithful to me,
and I pray that You will allow me
to become more faithful to You
in all ways and all times of my life.

Arise in Lowliness

*Arise My little one.
Arise to My call for humble simplicity,
Be lifted up to the joy of highest lowliness.*

One particular morning I was praying very much for a certain burden I carried in my heart: I felt so sorrowful over my continual lack of obedience to God. In my prayer time, I asked of the Lord over and over to please give me the grace for greater obedience to His will. I had been praying this way for awhile when He responded as though He hadn't heard the need that came from my heart.

Let Me speak to you about humility.

If you truly want to find Me – seek the place of humble presence. Seek to be free of self-focus, of self-glorification. People seek Me and then miss finding My presence because they assume My kingdom to be without lowly poverty. But I am well represented here – in humble love, humble acceptance, humble stillness. What is ordinary to you is profoundly rich, in simple humility, to Me. Why do you not see it? Because you want what the world seeks. Seek, instead, to find Me in all that is lowly – that is where everything of My kingdom dwells in harmony.

Learn how to love here – and you will learn to find the loving peace I wish for all My Church. Seek My presence in this way, and you will not be disappointed. The treasure you long to discover dwells there. I have made it so that no one, however poor, can be denied entrance. No one, however simple, can be unwelcomed. The treasure is here. Seek Me and find all that you need. How much I love My people.

Be small and unassuming. Let humble love be the treasure you seek. Don't deny yourself what I offer you today in My humble presence.

I pondered these words for a long time. It kept occurring to me that I had prayed for obedience and He only bid me to think about humility. Indeed, it is easier to be obedient when we become truly humble before Him.

> Lord, help me in all my needs – my need to be humble, my need for obedience to Your will, my need to grow in the desire for holiness. I so frequently miss the 'higher ground' You call me to dwell upon. I am truly grateful for Your constantly faithful and humbly present love.

How do we grow closer to God? I was thinking of this all day, since I heard it being discussed earlier among a group of people. I decided to ask the Lord in my prayer time, and He was gracious to answer me.

Arise in Lowliness

Begin with humility. David spoke from My heart when he said, "a humble and contrite heart you will not spurn." It will be the humble heart who hears My voice, and it will be the lowly ones who understand My ways. Those who thirst for Me, will receive the living waters I am so ready to pour out. Prepare your heart in this way: fast – pray – and wait upon Me in small things as well as matters of great importance. I alone see the significance of each detail in your life. All is of importance, and has far reaching consequences, when given to My eternal will. I have revealed to your heart already the place of sanctuary. It must be tended to in your own heart, for it is there you will find refuge in Me. There you will find peace, and there you will be sustained and nourished by My presence. How can man have so little faith when I have already revealed so much?

Lord, I want to hear Your voice and know Your ways. Increase my faith, especially in those areas where I doubt or fail to seek Your presence. Help me to be humble and lowly in my own heart, and so tend to the dwelling place where You can be received.

During the night, I was praying with such a great longing to be closer to God. Over and over I asked the Lord to let me come very near to Him. My desire for this was so deep, I could think of nothing else. I remembered then, as He had explained to me before, that such deep desires come to our heart *because we are*, in fact, *close to Him*, otherwise we would feel nothing for Him, nor would we even care for His presence or His love. The longing we have in our heart at these times is a part and a sharing of His own heart of love and longing for us.

I sat in His presence then, knowing I was being held in His heart. His love poured over my soul and filled me with gratitude and awe. It was strange to me that I felt such mixed stirrings in my heart then, for I suddenly knew that I was deeply loved, while, at the same time, I felt

Talitha Koum!

deeply 'unlovable'. My own unworthiness overwhelmed me, and I felt both close to God and far away from Him, as though my inadequacy and unworthiness could not accept His blessings. I was puzzled by the contradiction of emotions I carried inside.

I asked Him: Is my faith so weak that I cannot receive Your love and accept Your gracious caring for my needs?

His answer for me came that night in a dream: I saw myself standing outside, and very far off in the distance was a mountain. He asked me,

What appears to be larger, the mountain or yourself?

I answered: Myself, Lord. The mountain looks very small from here.

Then He let me see the mountain as though I was standing at its very base. Here the mountain was so large I could not even see its full height. He asked me again,

What appears to be larger now, the mountain or yourself?

The mountain, of course, is much greater.

Then He explained:

If you are far from Me, you only see yourself as prominent. When you draw very near, you are able to see your own neediness and dependency, even though you are near enough to feel My love at the same time. Remain very near to Me to see things as they are. But trust always in My provision and My constant love for you.

This gave me such joy and holy perspective, I thought of it many times over and it continues to fill me with gratitude and peace.

Arise in Lowliness

The Lord placed a further understanding of lowliness in my mind:

This was to consider the simplicity and lowliness of the present moment. How ordinary it looks to us, and how quickly we are ready to move on to something else, without fully appreciating God's purpose for the moment He has set before us. Each present second of life is important. If it were not so, we would not have it. The more we learn to live in the present – being fully present to Him – the more we will be equipped to embrace the future as it comes, for He has provided each moment with the necessary graces we need.

> Lord, I know I have lived too often in the past or in a misdirected longing for the future to come. I see, now, that I have ignored Your presence in my life many times by doing so. Please forgive me, and help me to graciously accept the holy purpose You have for me in each moment of my life.

I have pondered over and over the words on humility that I have heard. And I have seen for myself the beautiful humility and gracious simplicity that is in the Lord's heart. It caused me to ask Him:

> The more we experience Your presence, Lord, through extraordinary ways in our interior life, will it also be that we appear even more ordinary through outward ways in our exterior life? For it seems to me that what is extraordinary to You, Lord, seems very ordinary to the world.

To this question I only heard:

Humbleness will be the standard for My people.

Talitha Koum!

Then I recalled His earlier words to me:

Be small and unassuming. Let humble love be the treasure you seek. Don't deny yourself what I offer you today in My humble presence.

I am convinced, for the good of our soul, that we need to learn to live simply.

I encourage all of you who seek the Lord,
to ponder His humility
and how He has revealed Himself to you
in this simple and profound way.
Let us consider how we have responded
and embraced for ourselves
the call to humility in our own, personal way.

Arise in Me

Arise in Me, My daughter. Let all your life be a rising and a resting in Me.

I pray daily that I could grow in faithfulness, in patience, in forgiveness, in peace. I want to respond faithfully to the Lord's call, but I am painfully aware of my failings. Thankfully though, the Lord makes me gratefully aware that His love is sufficient to overcome my many weaknesses.

Let Me instruct you in a better way to live – to bring My healing and help to others, and to grow and ready yourself for eternity. You think it impossible to live the life of holiness and self-sacrifice. It is possible only through grace which I richly provide for at each need. I see what you cannot see – the inner working of your soul to grow and mature in My love. I provide for your soul's need. I provide patiently but faithfully. Your vision of this growth is inadequate, so humble trust is needed on your part, in place of understanding and clear vision. Acceptance and loving obedience is needed, in place of prideful action. Learn to wait upon Me. Learn from your choices – both the right and the

Talitha Koum!

wrong, for I am able to work everything together for good. Learn the joy of living in union with Me. Obedience, faith, and love open many doors.

I often just sit and think about the Lord's words to me. Over and over they go through my mind, and as this occurs, it seems that a small, almost imperceptible transformation starts to take place. It happens slowly, as I hear His words, as I dwell upon them, as I then believe and act in accord with them. I so want the joy of living in union with the Lord!

I do get so weary at times, and my repeated struggles only remind me that I am not living my life of faith as I should. It seems I come again and again to the Lord for help. I asked Him what I should do.

Be attentive to the conversion your soul needs. Be swift to hear, but slow to judge, and even more, slow to speak. Everyone, now, is in a time of discernment – a time to consider with sobering thoughtfulness – what is about them, and how they want to respond. Pray, and do not lose heart. Pray, and wait upon Me. Pray, and be changed – made new by My grace and your own choices for conversion.

> Lord, help me to embrace every opportunity You provide for my daily conversion. I see many opportunities after they have passed and I am sorry that I missed using them to grow closer to You. You are a faithful provider, Lord. Please provide for my needed change, and allow me to keep learning as I should. Thank You for Your constant love and help.

Arise in Me

Sometimes when the Lord speaks to my heart, it is a message that is especially comforting, or it is especially healing and peaceful. On other occasions, I sense that He wants to instruct me, or give me direction on how I may live in closer union to Him. At those times I make myself attentive to Him with concentrated focus. This was such a time.

My child, listen to My words of peace, My words of comfort, My words of longing for the Body – My Body waits for those who will listen and hear with emptiness of self – with ears undistracted, with wills turned only to My will and My longing for justice. My will, not the world's. My hope, not your distrust and doubting. Believe and stand firm in My words of life – and in My sacraments of truth. Know that it is I who call to your heart all the day long. If you will be still enough to listen and desiring enough to see My will fulfilled, you will find peace in your soul. I have left you the example to follow. Know that I am your God.

Later, He spoke with even greater need in His voice:

Come to My side, cling to Me, all who know Me. Come, stay close, stay very near. Your adversary does, indeed, prowl throughout the world seeking your ruin. But I am very near and remain in your midst to be your shield, your Savior. So few come close and stay in My presence, unless they feel a pressing need. Am I not your Lord at all times?

Comfort My heart that I may comfort yours. Do not look for Me with such preoccupation for worldly treasures, though I provide for all you need in the world. But even more, look to Me for Myself. Because My provision is complete, satisfying both present needs and eternal longings.

Come to Me, seeking first the kingdom of heaven, and other needs will be met with provision. I am the kingdom of heaven you seek. Why do so few people come to Me with their whole heart? Distractions of the world are leading you astray, when I have so much more to offer.

Talitha Koum!

I come, Lord. I come to know You and Your holy will for my life. Please help me, especially in those areas where I am drawn to worldly pleasures more than eternal truths. I want to seek You above all and love You with my whole heart.

I am learning to go to God for so many things now, that before I would not have thought to ask of Him. But, in truth, I still feel as though something is missing, because many times I do not have the peace after my prayers that I have known in the past. I think I must not be praying in the right way, or I am not praying enough.

These were my thoughts for many days, until one night when I was alone in my quiet time of prayer, the Lord spoke to me this answer:

You have given Me these needs and desires in your heart, but you still hold on to the timing of them. Release even that to Me, for My ways are not your ways and My timing is not your timing. I see all that needs to take place in the heavenly places and the earthly hearts. Before even a flower or fruit comes to its time of perfection, I have prepared it over weeks or months or years. I will answer your every need, but release it all to My perfect timing.

Increase my faith, Lord, especially in those areas where I still hold on, in some way, to what I prefer. Your design for my life is far better than my own. I give You my many needs and my desires; and I place the timing of Your perfect answer into Your faithful hands.

Arise in Me

Lord, I want to live in You – I want to fulfill Your will in my life, but sometimes I don't know if it is You or just myself and my own desires leading my thoughts.

When you feel it is My leading, prayerfully act upon it. When you are unsure, wait and move cautiously, but always pray. Prayer draws you to My side in deeper union because you are actively responding, but your action is toward Me, a deliberate choice to come into My will. See all your actions that way. Are they a moving toward My love, My holy presence, My will for you? Or, are they a moving of your own recognition? I will lead if you let Me. Do all for the glory of God and you will find rest for your soul.

Be at peace, My child, and let nothing disturb your peace, for I am at the center of it. I am the peace you call upon, the peace that sustains you, and the peace that brings all your actions into eternal good. Believe – be at peace – act from love.

My Lord, what if I don't have love, how can I act from what I do not feel inside of me?

Find the obstacle to loving and remove it. Is it un-forgiveness, fear, resentment? Find what hinders love from coming forth freely from your heart. Go back to faith, then, believing that I will help you in this step.

Re-center yourself in My peace and come back to My love. This is the fountain you must draw from for all you do. Apart from Me you can do nothing. People in a small village all know where to acquire the water they need to live. It is a well, or a river, or some source of water; and all go there.

You, too, know where your life-giving water is. Come to Me often. Come continuously. Come, knowing I am here to give you life and strength and ability.

Even when it seems you have the ability inside you, acknowledge Me for it, so that you are never separated from the source of good that is within you.

Talitha Koum!

Lord, I thank You for Your love that covers, heals, and strengthens me. May I learn to walk in this love and to love as You do.

The Lord knows all our needs,
all our thoughts, all our longings;
and He, alone, fulfills the purpose He has for us.
Today I pray that I can live in Him and with Him,
and faithfully rely on His strength and understanding.
I pray that all my actions will be
aligned to His will.

Arise and Serve

*Arise My daughter, and serve
those who need to find Me.*

The Lord, I have learned, calls us to become like Him – like Him in love, like Him in forgiveness, like Him in patience, faithfulness, meekness … like Him in all ways. The 'likeness' I need to work on especially is to be like Him in serving others.

My child, it is in the very humblest state, the lowliest place of the heart that you are able to hear My heart – My heart for the poor, for the oppressed, for the down-trodden, for all who are hurting. I am near to the broken-hearted; I hear the cries of the needy. I am always loving you, My child, but I am always hearing the cries of My children in need. Will you come close enough to listen as I listen, and serve them as I would serve?

Talitha Koum!

I want to hear, Lord, as You hear, and to love as You love. My heart feels so small when it comes to loving deeply and sincerely. I know You can help me with this. I trust that You are increasing the capacity of my small heart so that I can bear more love and bring more loving care to others. Make my small heart to be like Your very great, compassionate heart, Lord.

Sometimes I look at people and see so much emptiness. Some are empty because they have nothing, and others are empty because they have too much of all that is meaningless. And we who know the Lord should be able to help them somehow. I, myself, fail at this so many times; I say I will do one thing, and then I do another.

> Lord, do You truly continue to love us when we repeatedly let You down? I don't know how we can help others find faith in You, when we need greater faithfulness ourselves. Help us to love You sincerely and to have a faithful heart for loving those You put into our life. Do not deny us Your love, Lord, even when we fail to embrace it as we should.

My child, the love in My heart is forever. Why do you doubt it? I create in love. I am – Myself – love. Help those who do not understand My love for them. Bring them closer. Let them see your love of Me through your loving care of their needs. All who love Me – all who are filled with the love I pour out, and the graces I provide through My Holy Spirit – should reflect this healing love to others. Do not question that I want you to be an instrument of My loving care. The hurting, the sorrowful, the needy must receive not just the prayers for inner healing, but the outward signs, which come forth through those who are faithful witnesses of My love. Bring others to this love whenever possible. Explain in words of comfort and actions of service, what My love longs to provide: healing, help, restoration, peace, mercy, new life. My kingdom is at hand – rejoice and be glad. But live as though you know My kingdom in a very present way, so others will be able to see and believe.

There is so great a need in our world for people to know the Lord. They do not see what we, who believe, can see. They do not receive into their hearts what we have received. I brought this heaviness in my heart to Him in prayer.

My Lord, what can one person do to bring so much to so many in need? I feel too small and inadequate to make a difference. What would You have me do?

People will need something to hold onto. Your faith can help them. Let them see your steadfast love and confident trust in Me. Do not doubt that I am working My perfect will through your simple acts of love and mercy and patient endurance. Embrace all with the unity you have witnessed of My kingdom. Perfect love casts out fear; stay near to Me to be filled with this love. Will you trust so that others can see and rejoice in My love and faithfulness? I will bring about the transformation needed.

Lord, I will continue on this path of faith and trust in You. I believe that You will bring about the needed transformation — in my own soul — and in the souls of others. Your way is perfect and Your love is perfect. Thank You for the gift of witnessing to Your kingdom of love.

I am learning to become much more sensitive to the Lord's heart in my prayer times with Him. I can sometimes feel, within myself, a small portion of the immense love He has for His people. How much He longs to speak to them and comfort them, and bring them into His care. He gives to all so freely, and He waits for His love to be received and shared

and lived among us. I pray to grow more like Him in my love for others. But when it is hard to love the person that is before me as I should, I have to remember that He is within that person, and I am truly loving Him in their poor need.

"Will you listen to the cries of My Body – My people – who are hurting and dying? I have all in My hands to give – to heal and to make new. Who will listen and be conformed to My living Word that healing and help can come?"

Lord, I want to be conformed to Your image, and bring Your love to those You call me to serve. Help me to look beyond my discomfort, and let me remember that You call me to be a servant like You. They are Your loved ones, Lord, and when I am loving them, I am loving You. When I am serving them, I am serving You. Change my heart, please, that I would desire and do what is needed to carry Your comfort and care to others.

I often look upon my own needs and forget, or ignore, the needs of those around me. I know this is not the way of God's kingdom. Self-focus hinders our well-being in so many ways. I am trying to learn to walk in His way of holy surrender, and leave behind my attachments to the world. Help me, Lord, in this.

Do you desire to be with Me? I am already here. Do you desire to receive My help for your needs? My grace is already abundantly present. You, however, are the one who chooses where you will place your attention – on My kingdom or on the world.

Arise and Serve

Lord, I realize that most of my thoughts and actions are filled with self-focus, but I ask You to bring me to the depth of love that will make my desire and attention be for You and for others. Please fill me with the purity of love that reflects Your way of humble service.

It seems more and more to me that the most important and worthwhile thing we can do in our life is to glorify God by growing in holiness and by helping and inspiring others to do the same. I pray that God will be praised in all I do and say today.

Live in My kingdom, child. My kingdom is the kingdom of My presence, My peace, My love, My grace. Always you are equipped with grace in My presence – always you are held in love. Bring others to this place of holy presence and learn to remain in it yourself. From now on, listen with new ears, and let yourself feel with new depth of love. Walk in new patience and forgiveness. Speak with new understanding, feel with new compassion. Cry with new tears. Offer to others a new depth of being – the being of presence in Me. I have shared all of this with you, as it comes through the heart of selfless giving.

If you follow Me, if you lose your life, if you give up all for love of Me, you will surely find the holy kingdom of My presence, and you will have all that is needed. You will be equipped for joyful service and abundant life. Live in Me.

I come, Lord, to Your holy and loving heart to ask that You make mine like Your own. I want to live in Your presence and in Your kingdom of love. I know I cannot do this without being made as one with You. Allow me, Lord, to let You fashion this holy love upon my heart.

Talitha Koum!

The Lord's words to me have made me consider many things in a different light. I can see that my desire to be of humble service is a great gift, a gift that I can use to benefit others and serve God's will. Jesus was a servant. This is so beyond our way of understanding – to see God as a servant, but, as I am learning, this is the way of love.

My little one, how I long to heal the hearts that are wounded. Bring them to Me in your prayers, in your confident faith and your words of hope-filled praise. The time you spend in prayer is time spent with Me – placing the cares of your heart into My heart. Is there any need I cannot handle? Then place all in My heart and trust in My loving provision. How completely I want to heal and restore all to wholeness. I wait for your requests, your confident leaning on Me to answer. I wait for your love to seek Me above all.

Lord, I want Your love to fill my life and change me into a more loving servant – one that serves You through my prayers, my actions, and my words. I see so many hurting people and I want to help them in greater ways. Please show me how. You, Lord, care for these hurting ones even more than I do. Help me to live in You and bring to them Your help.

Today I ask that I could grow in purer love for others.
I pray that I could look upon those I meet this day
and truly see the Lord. He is there – loving them –
but often with a broken heart from
the heaviness He feels in their need.
Help me, Lord, to serve and love
and bring to others Your kindness,
as You have so lovingly shown it to me.

Arise in My Love

*Arise now. Arise in My love
and bring My love to others.*

When we grow closer to God, we do not necessarily see the growth our soul is making. Sometimes we assume great growth is there, when we are very much lacking in it; and other times we do not see any advancement at all, while it shines very brightly before the Lord. What is best, I think, is to serve the Lord quietly and without assumptions, keeping our minds on the Lord, and less on ourselves. Then we can be all the more grateful when some progress is made.

My child, you bless Me in your presence here. You bless Me in your acts of love and gentleness. You bless Me in your prayers of devotion and your prayers of intercession. You bless and bring comfort to Me in your desires and striving to grow in holiness. It is My will that we be one, and it is My will that you draw others ever nearer to My Sacred Heart. Pray and be filled with the graces I pour forth for your soul to receive. Lead others to the portals of faith. Grace abounds, but few receive. Pray, and bring to others the

understanding of My love and mercy. Pray, and teach others to believe. Pray, and wait upon My leading. By the power of the Holy Spirit, all things will fall into place for you as you seek to serve My will. Faith, hope, and love at all times.

Lord, I do not thank You enough for creating me to be one with You. I do not consider enough the great gift You offer me to live in You and You in me. Fill me, Lord, with this love, and help me to bring this great gift of Your love to others.

I am so grateful for these quiet times of prayer I have with the Lord. Without them, I would not know the Lord's love or the peace-filled ways of His kingdom. But I continually discover that there is much more to know, so much more to comprehend.

Lord, Your ways are beyond our understanding, Your wisdom is truly foolishness to this world. How do we dare ask for this wisdom and understanding to fill us? How could we, who are so foolish ourselves, begin to hear and comprehend what Your perfect wisdom contains? Help us to hear and know and live in truth.

I will tell you how to hear My voice: stillness, desire, and persistent attention to love. Bring your cares to Me and see yourself in My loving presence. I am eager to be with you, but worldly matters fill your attention instead of longing for Me. When I am made the center – the love and desire of your heart – I am present to fill the soul's deepest need. Empty of the world's focus, your heart can receive a heavenly focus, and I am present to fill your heart. Sing of My love.

Thank You, Lord, for leading Your people with such love. Keep us near to You and enable us to live truly as Your children. May we become children who seek and listen to Your words of love and guidance.

I confess that I was deeply distressed today over a matter among old acquaintances. I was having a hard time getting past the frustration and anger that was in my heart. After many hours and much anxiety, the Lord spoke to my heart:

My patient, loving one, come to Me with these needs and let Me help you.

> Lord, You know better than I that I am neither patient, nor loving, especially at this time. Why address me in this way?

I call forth what needs to be, My child. I am giving you the grace to become patient and loving. The more you think of yourself in these terms, the more quickly you will grow in imitating them.

Then, in my heart, I felt the love He was offering, and it began to change my feelings and attitude. I thanked the Lord, and I wanted even more to praise Him for this grace that I was newly aware of, the grace that was changing me interiorly.

> May You, Lord, be praised at all times of my life! How wonderful to think that my small life can be an instrument of praise to You!

I think it should give our hearts great delight to praise our Lord. How many times before I have not chosen to, or even thought of, praising Him with my life. But each day I have that opportunity.

> Lord, I offer everything I do to You in praise and thanksgiving. Let me live each moment to see You glorified. May Your love always fill me and enable me to give You honor, glory, and praise! Thank You, gracious Lord.

Talitha Koum!

My time in prayer was very different this morning. There seemed to be a serious presence about the Lord, as though He was going to speak to me about something of special importance. I asked how I should pray, as I sensed a need for my closest attention.

Sit with Me. My heart is heavy with sorrow, heavy with sorrow. You ask Me how to pray at this time of deep need. I see the hearts of all who suffer, but few understand that those hearts live in Me, in a way you have yet to perceive with depth and clarity. I bear them all and suffer with them, but more keenly, because I see the hope and comfort that could be theirs, but, for lack of faith, is missing. Pray for faith at this time of great need. Pray for comfort to be received. Pray for perseverance and patience and the love I have poured out for all – to be received into empty hearts. All the world is undergoing a deep conversion process. Will you pray for hearts to receive at this time, the hope that turns them to Me? Let hearts be encouraged. There are many who see what is happening with faith – many more who are called to deepen their faith. Many who are seeking, but need your prayers to get them through. Encourage whenever you have the opportunity. Many will say, "I cannot see God." But those who are keeping their hearts steadfast in Me will find rest for their souls. These faithful ones must keep vigil for those whose faith is weak. Pray – and keep your hearts close to My Sacred Heart. So much remains to be done, but all have a part in My plan of hope and restoration. Think not that I have abandoned those in need. I am exposing the needs that are deeply hidden, so that healing can come. Light is shining now in darkened places. Pray that truth and comfort are received and let love be seen among My people as a bright light that directs all back to Me. How much I love. How much I love. Stay with Me that My love can continue to fill you, direct you, and transform your thoughts, your heart, your whole being.

I come to sit with You, Lord, and I pray for all who suffer, especially those who suffer because they do not know You. I pray that I could always respond to Your heart of love with obedience, and bring Your comfort and light to those in need. Help me, please, to do this.

God's love continues to deepen in my heart, so that I can clearly see I am different inside now than I was a year ago. I don't distain the struggles that come with loving others as I used to do. I don't complain as I did so often before when my circumstances call me to bear some sorrow or pain over another person's actions. The Lord has shown me that in the very hardest time of loving others, the mystery of love's power can work profoundly within our hearts.

This, my child, is where you join in their struggle. Do you understand the invitation of this great gift? It is the gift of life in Me – life that is overflowing with love, and love in all its willingness to be long-suffering – love that reaches beyond your human comprehension – love that gives of itself for the good of the other. Never cease to grow in this love. Never cease to be transformed and made new by its power. I long to transform the world with My love.

———◆———

This love is not easy, but it seems to come with its own inner strength that makes everything more bearable, even, at times, to the point of bearing difficult things with joy. I find myself willingly sharing in the pain and struggles of others for love of them. This is a great change in myself! How God does such a transforming work, I cannot understand. But I thank Him profusely for it.

Talitha Koum!

As I contemplated the great love that is in God's heart, I felt as if a window had been opened in my understanding, and through this window I saw that love held three particular joys for us. The first joy is in *knowing* God's love. This is the beginning of our perception of what His love means, how pure and holy, and generously abundant it is. We perceive that we are the object of God's love, though we cannot earn or comprehend it. His love is freely given and we joyfully and thankfully receive.

The second joy is *sharing* God's love. This is more than the delight of knowing that He loves us. This is the deeper communion of growing in this love with God. We were created to share this love in deep intimacy with Him. What great joy this brings to our soul. This is a personal exchange of His love with our love, which is made, to the best of our ability, in purity, depth, and gratitude.

But third is the greatest joy of all: it is that of *becoming* God's love. This is the joy of being united to the Lord in bringing His love to other people. In this joy, pure love frees us of self attachment, and we know the deeper fulfillment of living for others.

I think that once we perceive His love and begin to walk in it, we are gradually more able to embrace it ourselves. Then, over time and grace, it becomes a part of our nature. How blessed we are to have God's love and joy offered so freely to us. How blessed we are to become that love and offer it to others by God's grace.

> Lord, how gently and how sweetly You invite us to this love! Let me learn to live and walk in Your love throughout my day. And in all the days that make up my life, let me live completely in You. Teach me, Lord, how to love as You love.

Arise in My Love

On one morning, after a particularly joyous time of opening my heart to the Lord in prayer, He said to me,

I want you to become a living-carving of My love.

I did not completely understand this, so He added,

Some must be asleep as I carve my love upon them.

By this I was shown that He was referring to people who must be unconscious of what He is doing. As His desire is to draw us into union with Him – and union with Him means a union with *purest love* – we must often be unaware of this divine intention because *this love* – we would discover – is too deep for us to bear. Our sensitivity is so naturally directed to ourselves, until we begin to outgrow self-focused inclinations. Therefore, as our Lord begins to carve His love upon our souls, we can neither understand nor embrace it with any great depth. We learn, instead, to grow in faith, hope, and love of Him. And in doing so, God leads our souls along this path of ever-deepening-love.

As He was explaining these things to me, a vivid memory, then, began to make this even more clear. I remembered as a child, watching a man in our village as he skillfully worked on a piece of wood – cutting, carving, and shaping it. How hard it was to cut in certain places. How long it took before the wood began to take on a new shape. How patient the man was in working with it, seeing only in his own mind the beautiful image still hidden beneath the surface of the wood.

In recalling this memory, I suddenly understood that we are all like that piece of wood that I saw being transformed before my eyes – only we are *alive*, so we *feel* every impression the master carpenter is making upon us. We feel every edge He is taking off and every new line or curve He has to cut in order to make His desired image come forth. The man I saw in my childhood who shaped that piece of wood, was not working on something that could feel his cutting and carving. I imagine it would have been impossible to carve at all if that piece of wood could have resisted the woodcutter's attempts.

But this is how I was shown the great gift we posses in our free will. In our gift of free will we can see how greatly we honor God in using it *for Him*. We *do feel* the transformation that must take place. And *we can resist* the cutting and shaping of our souls. But we can also cooperate with God's creating hand, and if we trust the Lord and remain pliable to His fashioning of us, we become as He asked of me in prayer – a living and faithful *carving of His love*. To become a *'living-carving'* means to become sensitively docile and fully interacting with God's fashioning of our soul, no matter how difficult or painful it seems. This love – that is God – needs to become the deepest part of our nature. It is *pure* love, and cannot be pure within us unless it is freely given and freely received, so we have *free will* as our first steps of learning how to freely love. What glory and delight this gives our Lord when we use our own will to trust Him and love Him. I want to learn to love in this way. I want the Lord to look upon my soul and take great delight in fashioning it to his own likeness of love.

As I was made aware of this free-will gift, I began to pray that I would never resist the carving of my own soul. I pray still that I can give glory to God in every way He chooses to deepen my ability and sensitivity to love. Learning to love selflessly means learning surrender – the trust and surrender that allows His work of grace to move unhindered in my life.

These words continue to grow within me. It is my daily prayer that I could do as He asks.

Thank You, Lord, for leading me with true and constant guidance; thank You for the gift of faith that allows me to trust in Your love. I give You my heartfelt longings, Lord, and ask You to inspire me with greater love to live according to Your will. Keep me always in an attitude of trust and surrender, and help me to remember Your faithfulness when difficulties come. Make it my desire to be one with You in all things.

As we daily come before God's presence in prayer,
everything in our heart and mind
is filled more perfectly with His love.
His pure and holy love inspires us
to live in Him and serve others,
as He does so humbly and willingly.
Lord, let me be filled with desire and inspiration
to become like You in all ways.
Fashion my soul into Your image of love.

Talitha Koum!

I think back many times to those days of my childhood. When I was growing up, I loved the fact that everyone knew me as Jairus' daughter, 'the little girl Jesus raised from the dead.' I would hear people tell the story to visitors who came to our city. Sometimes people traveled great distances to meet me, and I would hear my father explain the same story to everyone who asked. I was very happy that people knew I had a special relationship with Jesus.

But my father used to tell me, "Don't get bigheaded over this, my daughter – for Jesus raises many from death to life. That is why He came."

My father was right, of course. The Lord still does this miracle - daily - for anyone who believes. He brings new life to all who answer His call:

Arise My loved one. Arise to new life in Me.

But to all who received Him,
who believed in His name,
He gave power to become children of God;
who were born, not of blood
nor of the will of the flesh
nor of the will of man,
but of God.
John 1:12-13

[1] Mark 5:22-24, 35-41a

[2] Psalm 34:1, 3

[3] Psalm 32:6

[4] Psalm 28:7

[5] Psalm 35:17

Talitha Koum

in some translations: Talitha cumi.

Talitha Kuom - pronounced: tal-ee-thah koom

The critical Greek text reads talitha kum in Mark 5:41; the received text talitha kumi is grammatically accurate but represents an editorial correction. The Greek is a transliteration of the Aramaic (words) meaning, "maiden, stand up."

   Dictionary of the Bible, John L. McKenzie, S.J.
   New York: Bruce Publishing Company, 1965. 866.

If you would like more information about the author, or would be interested in contacting her, she can be reached through her website:

jerryandcricketaull.com